Graphs, Graphs, Graphs!

by Kelly Boswell

CAPSTONE PRESS
a capstone imprint

A+ Books are published by Capstone Press,
1710 Roe Crest Drive, North Mankato, Minnesota 56003
www.capstonepub.com

Library of Congress Cataloging-in-Publication Data
Boswell, Kelly.
Graphs, graphs, graphs! / by Kelly Boswell.
pages cm. — (A+ books. Displaying information)
Audience: K to grade 3.
Summary: "Introduces types of graphs and how they are used"—Provided by publisher.
Includes index.
ISBN 978-1-4765-0259-5 (library binding)
ISBN 978-1-4765-3336-0 (paperback)
ISBN 978-1-4765-3340-7 (ebook PDF)
1. Graphic methods—Juvenile literature. 2. Correlation (Statistics)—Juvenile literature. I. Title.
 QA90.B663 2014
 001.4'226—dc23   2012050479

Editorial Credits
Kristen Mohn, editor; Juliette Peters, designer; Marcie Spence, media researcher;
Charmaine Whitman, production specialist

Photo Credits
Capstone Studio: Karon Dubke, 1, 4, 6, 7, 8, 9, 10, 11 (bottom), 12, 13, 14–15, 16, 17, 18, 19, 20,
23, 24, 25, 26–27, 28–29, 32; Shutterstock: caesart, cover (bottom), Coprid, cover (middle left),
jane87, 11 (top), Kim Reinick, cover (top), 3, Samo Trebizan, cover (middle), Suslik1983, cover
(middle right)

Metric Conversion
1 inch=2.54 centimeters
90 degrees Fahrenheit=32.2 degrees Celsius

Note to Parents, Teachers, and Librarians
This Displaying Information book uses full color photographs and a nonfiction format to
introduce the concept of graphs. This book is designed to be read aloud to a pre-reader or
to be read independently by an early reader. Photographs help listeners and early readers
understand the text and concepts discussed. The book encourages further learning by
including the following sections: Table of Contents, Glossary, Read More, Internet Sites,
and Index. Early readers may need assistance using these features.

Printed in the United States of America in North Mankato, Minnesota.
032013   007223CGF13

Table of Contents

What Is a Graph?

Graphs are pictures that help us organize and understand things around us.

We use graphs to share information with others. We also use graphs to see how things change over time.

Graphs use bars, pictures, lines, or parts of circles to compare things.

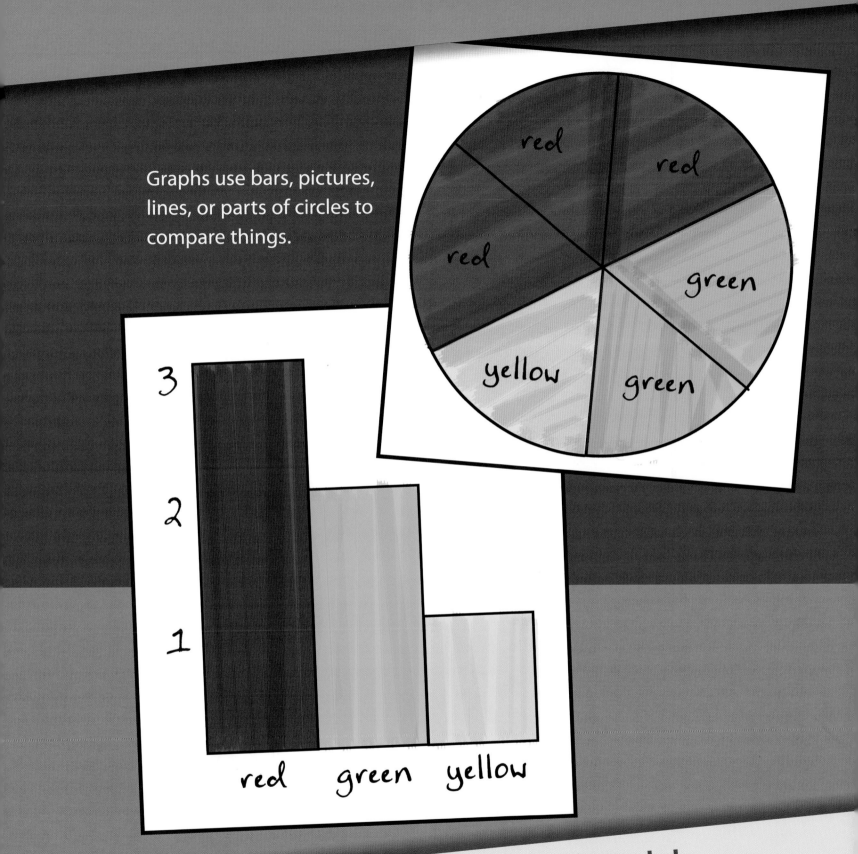

Let's see what graphs can do!

Pictographs

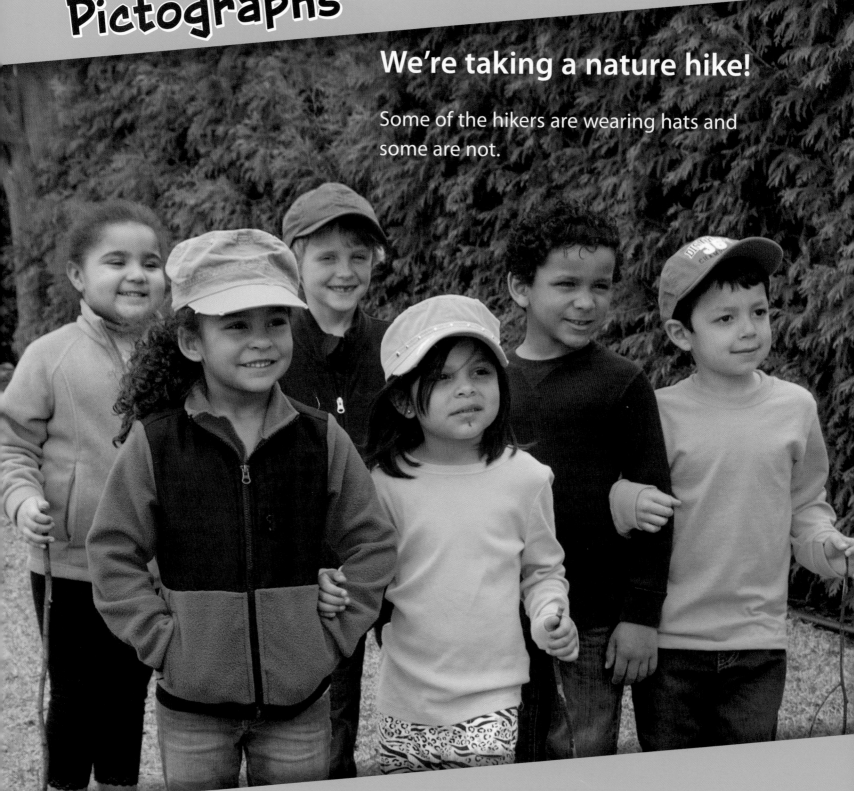

We're taking a nature hike!

Some of the hikers are wearing hats and some are not.

Let's line up each group of hikers.

Which row is longer?

We can use pictures to compare.

We'll make a pictograph.

The key at the bottom shows that each picture stands for one child. Our pictograph shows that more kids are wearing hats.

What are the hikers wearing on their feet?
Let's show their shoes in a pictograph.

The children are wearing flip-flops, boots, and tennis shoes. The pictures help us compare. More of the children are wearing tennis shoes.

 = tennis shoes

 = boots

 = flip-flops

Go change your shoes, Alice!

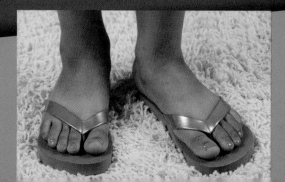

Bar Graphs

We collected all kinds of treasures on our nature hike! We can sort the treasures into groups.

Let's line them up.
Then we can compare.

Which group has the most?

Bar graphs compare the amount of each kind of something.

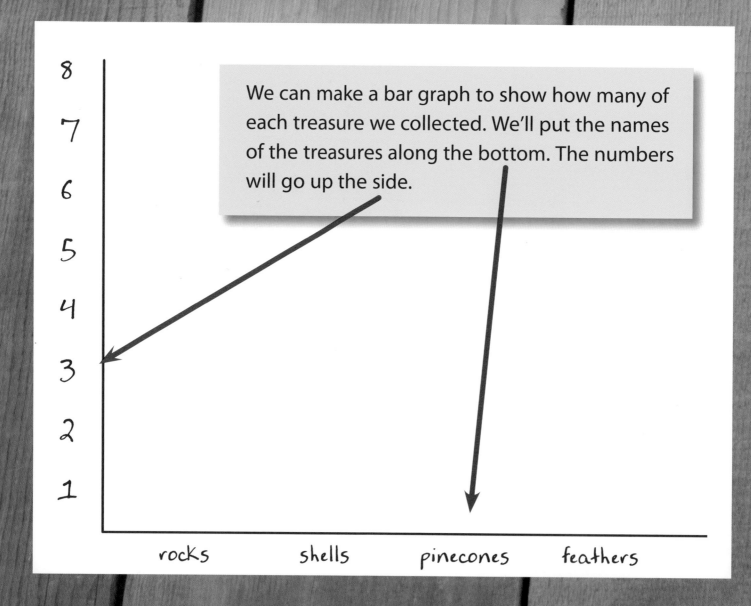

We can make a bar graph to show how many of each treasure we collected. We'll put the names of the treasures along the bottom. The numbers will go up the side.

Key

■ = rocks

■ = shells

■ = pinecones

■ = feathers

Let's give each of our treasures a color. We will use gray to show the rocks. Shells will be blue. Pinecones will be brown, and feathers will be tan. The key shows what each color stands for.

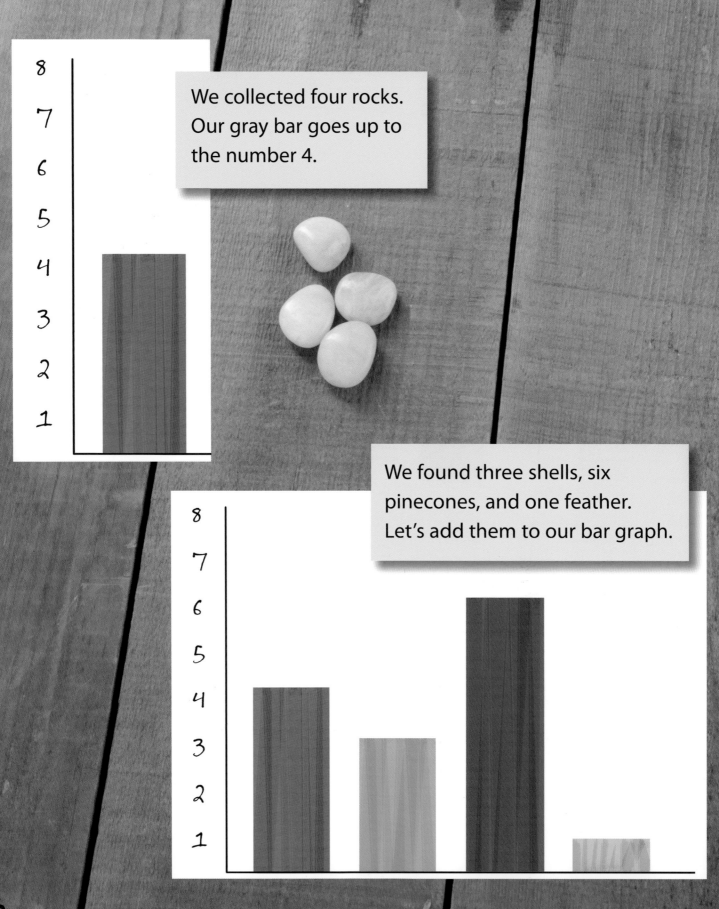

We collected four rocks. Our gray bar goes up to the number 4.

We found three shells, six pinecones, and one feather. Let's add them to our bar graph.

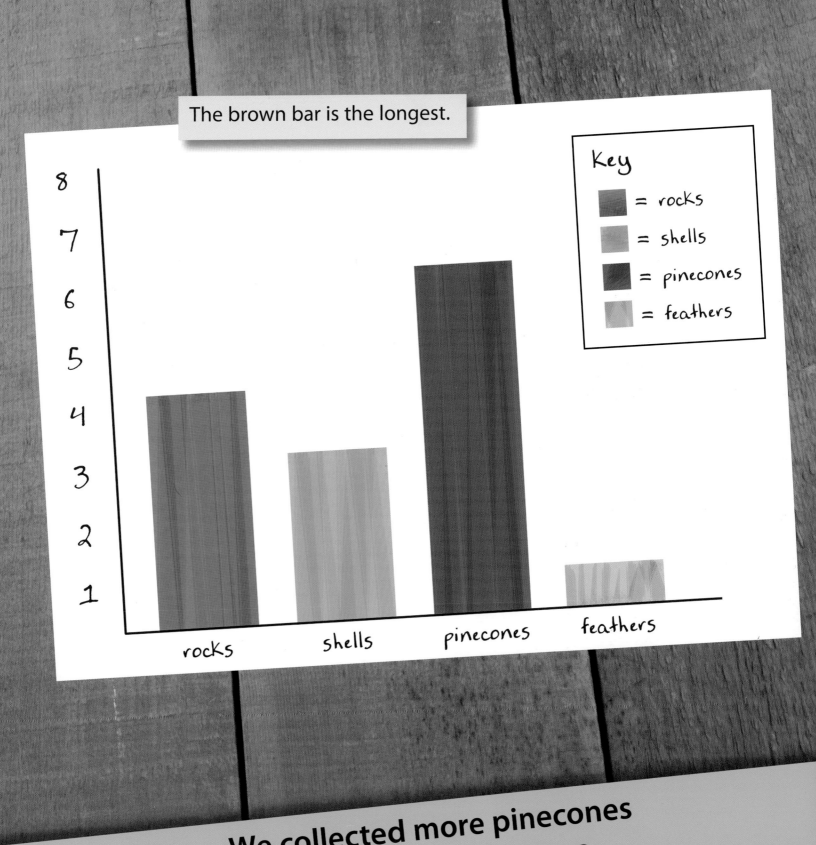

The brown bar is the longest.

Key

= rocks

= shells

= pinecones

= feathers

8

7

6

5

4

3

2

1

rocks   shells   pinecones   feathers

We collected more pinecones
than any other treasure.

Line Graphs

Sam knows exercise helps him grow. Each month Sam records how tall he is.

Is Sam getting taller?

We can make a line graph to show how Sam is growing.

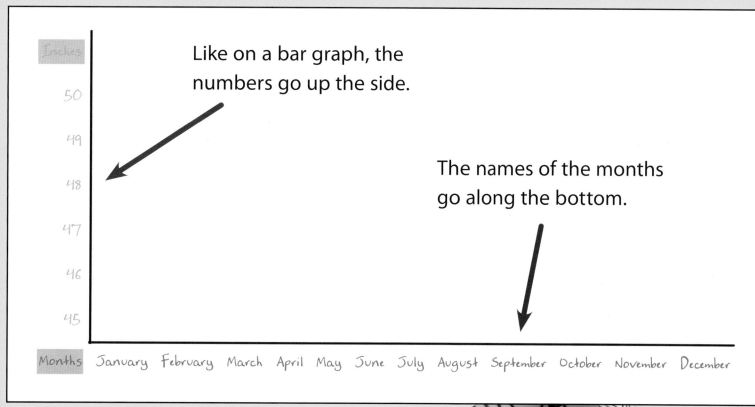

Like on a bar graph, the numbers go up the side.

The names of the months go along the bottom.

Inches

50
49
48
47
46
45

Months | January | February | March | April | May | June | July | August | September | October | November | December

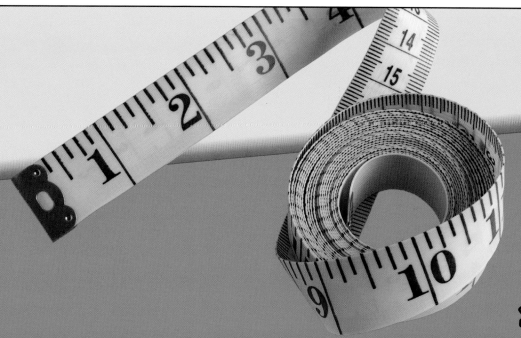

We make dots to show Sam's height each month. Then we connect the dots.

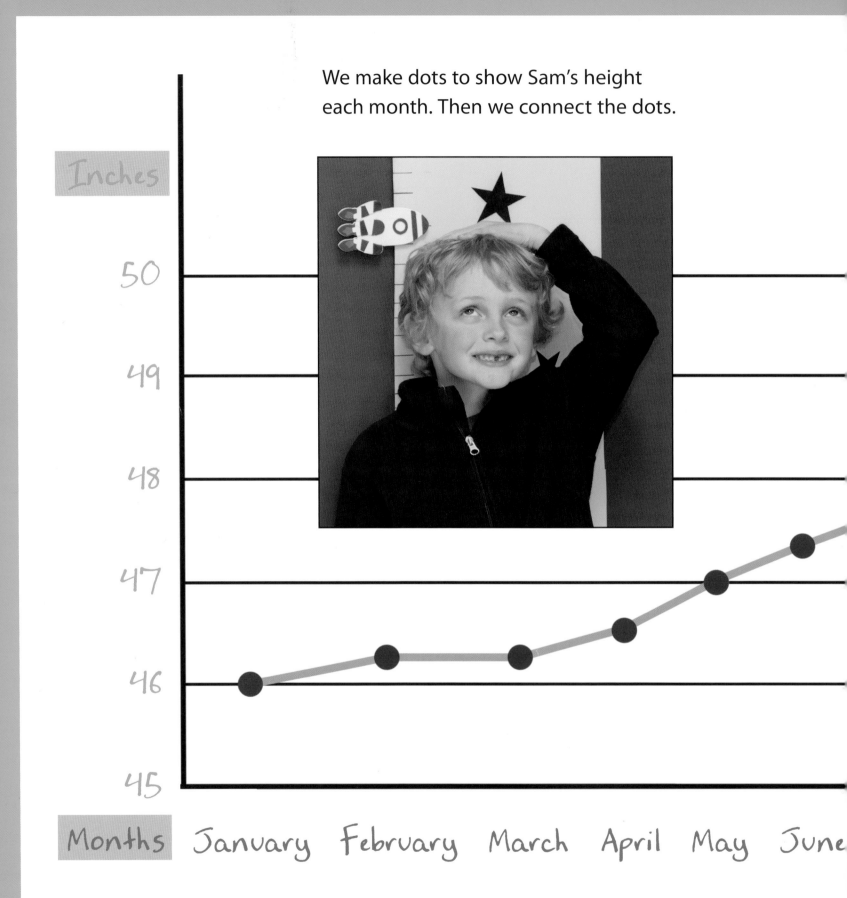

Inches

50

49

48

47

46

45

Months January February March April May June

A line graph helps us see the
change in Sam's height over time.

Sam grew 3 inches this year!

July   August   September   October   November   December

How's the weather? This line graph shows the temperature for each day in a month. Follow the line to see how the temperature changed over time.

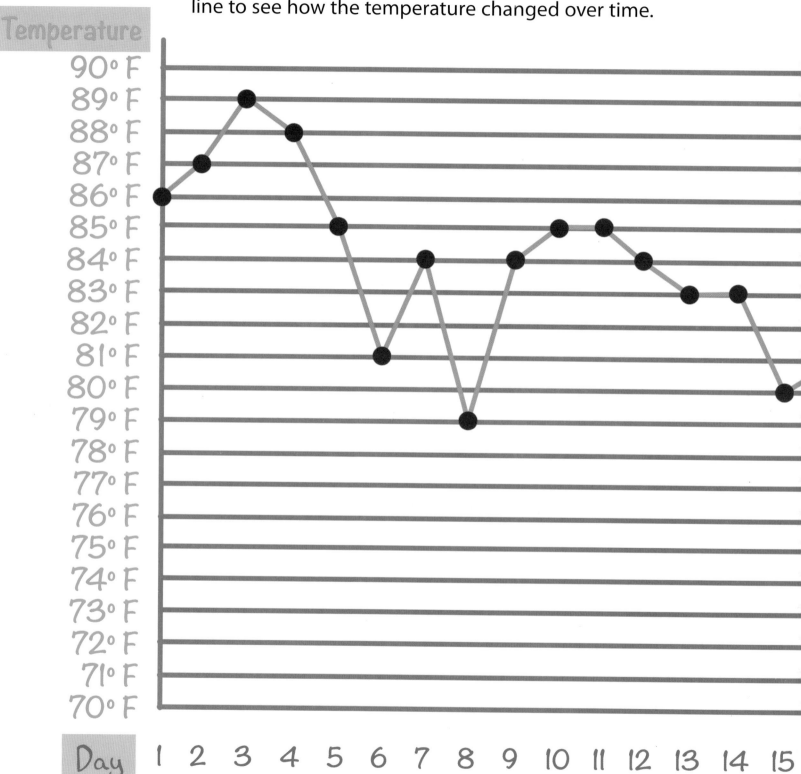

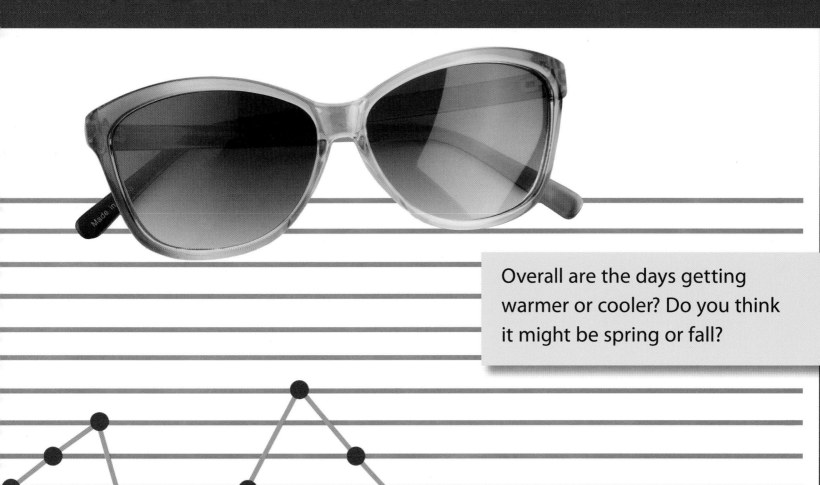

Overall are the days getting warmer or cooler? Do you think it might be spring or fall?

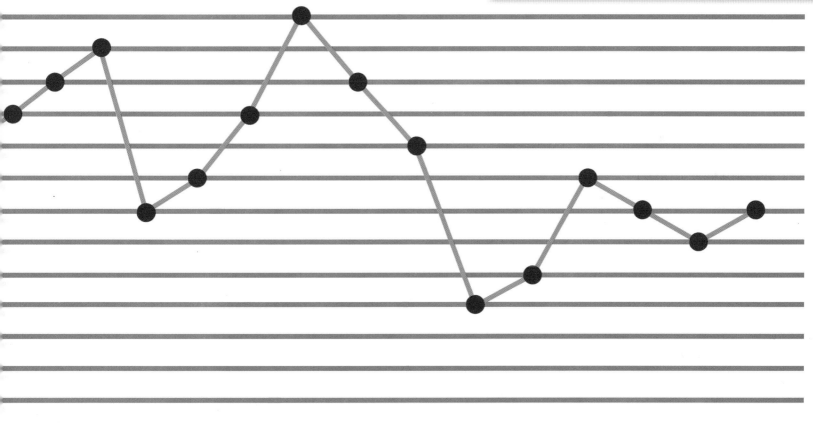

6 17 18 19 20 21 22 23 24 25 26 27 28 29 30

Pie Graphs

Exercise makes you hungry!

Three of the hikers share a pizza for lunch.
They cut the pizza into eight equal pieces.

Let's Eat!

The friends each take some pizza. A pie graph can show how much is taken and how much is left.

The circle stands for the whole pizza. The red part shows how much was eaten. The blue part shows how much is left.

Pie graphs show how parts compare to the whole.

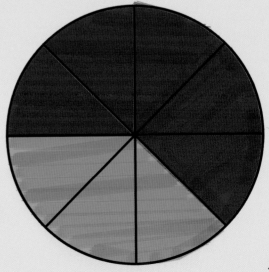

A pie graph can also show how much pizza each friend ate. This circle has five equal parts. That's one part for each piece of pizza that was eaten.

key
■ = Alice
□ = José
■ = DeShawn

The key shows a different color for each friend. Alice and José each ate two slices. DeShawn ate one slice. **Yum!**

It's berries for dessert! Try sorting the berries in different ways. Your graph will look different if you sort them by color, type of berry, or votes for favorite berry.

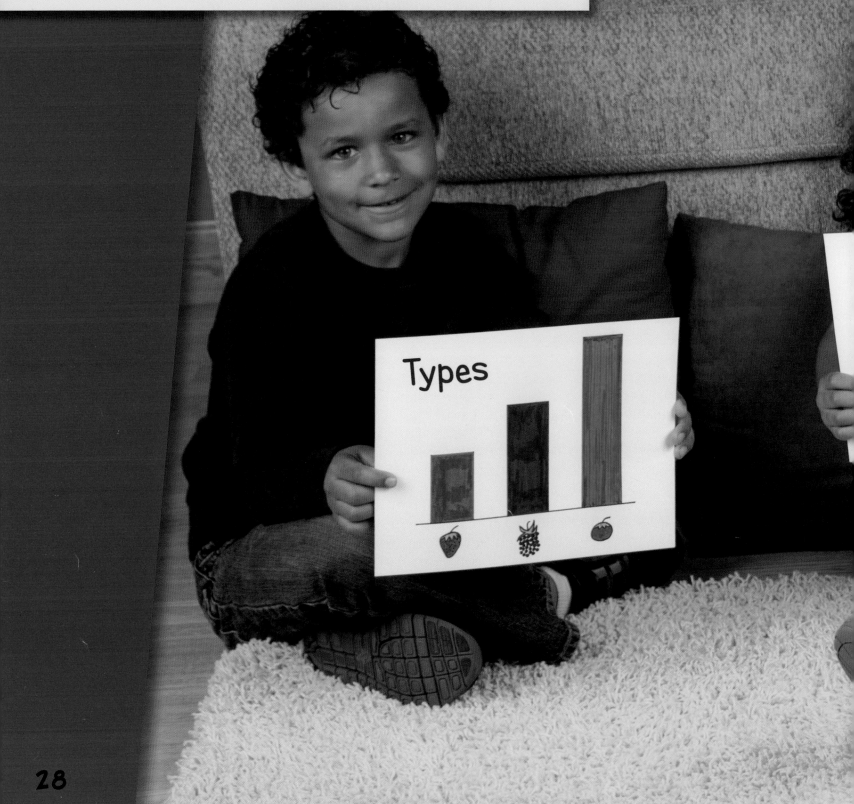

How would you graph these berries?

Glossary

bar—a long, flat, block shape; on a graph, the taller or longer the bar, the more of something you have

compare—to judge one thing against another

equal—the same as something else in size, number, or value

graph—a picture that compares numbers or amounts; graphs use bars, lines, pictures, or parts of circles to compare

key—a list or chart that explains symbols on a graph

row—a line of things arranged side by side

Critical Thinking Using the Common Core

1. The two graphs on page 5 show the same information. Explain how they are alike and different. (Craft and Structure)

2. Look at the children on page 7. Now look at the graph on page 9. Explain the way in which the children match the diagram. (Integration of Knowledge and Ideas)

3. Study the graph on pages 22 and 23. What was the coldest day of the month? Which day was the warmest? (Key Ideas and Details)

Read More

Nelson, Robin *Let's Make a Picture Graph.* First Step Nonfiction—Graph It! Minneapolis: Lerner Publications, Co., 2013.

Piddock, Claire. *Line, Bar, and Circle Graphs.* New York: Crabtree, 2010.

Taylor-Butler, Christine. *Understanding Charts and Graphs.* A True Book. New York: Children's Press, 2012.

Internet Sites

FactHound offers a safe, fun way to find Internet sites related to this book. All of the sites on FactHound have been researched by our staff.

Here's all you do:

Visit *www.facthound.com*

Type in this code: 9781476502595

 Check out projects, games and lots more at **www.capstonekids.com**

Index